MORE PROBLEM PLAYS

By the same author

PROBLEM PLAYS
EIGHT PLAYS TO FINISH
MORE PLAYS TO FINISH
A FIRST BOOK OF ACTION PLAYS

First published in Great Britain 1984
by Hulton Educational Publications Ltd
Old Station Drive, Leckhampton,
CHELTENHAM, GL53 0DN, England

© *Ann Farquhar-Smith* 1984

Reprinted 1988

ISBN 0 7175 1228 2

Phototypeset in 11/13pt Times by Input Typesetting Ltd, London
SW19 8DR

Printed in Hong Kong by Wing King Tong Co. Ltd

MORE

PROBLEM PLAYS

Ann Farquhar-Smith

Hulton Educational

CONTENTS

PARENTS

We Gave Her Most of our Lives

Characters

MANDY RICHARDSON
MR RICHARDSON
MRS RICHARDSON
CLIVE
LISA
STEVE

We Gave Her Most of our Lives

Scene I

At the Richardsons' house
Mandy, Mr and Mrs Richardson

MANDY: I'm off, Mum.

MRS RICHARDSON: No, you're not. Come in here and let's take a look at you.

MANDY: Mum, I'll be late!

MR RICHARDSON: You heard what your mother said—let's take a look at you.

MRS RICHARDSON: Just as I thought. You're not going out of my house dressed like that.

MANDY: Like what?

MRS RICHARDSON: Look at you. That hair for a start. How did you get it that colour?

MANDY: It's only a rinse. It'll wash out. Warren's hair is much worse and it's permanent.

MR RICHARDSON: You leave Warren out of this. Go upstairs this minute and wash that stuff out of your hair. And while you're at it, you can take that muck off your face.

MANDY: Oh, Dad, it's only make-up. Everybody wears make-up like this these days.

MR RICHARDSON: No daughter of mine is going out of this house with that on her face.

MRS RICHARDSON: And that skirt! Just look at the length of that skirt!

MANDY: What's wrong with my skirt? Everybody's wearing them this length. It's the fashion.

MRS RICHARDSON: I suppose if the fashion was wearing newspapers you'd follow it. Now get upstairs and change.

MR RICHARDSON: We don't want you back down here until you're decent.

MANDY: But I am decent. There's nothing wrong with what I'm wearing. All my friends go out looking like this.

MRS RICHARDSON: That doesn't make it right for you. Just because your friends go out looking like trollops, that's no excuse for you dressing like one yourself.

MANDY: Oh, Mum, just this once. It's Lisa's birthday party.

MRS RICHARDSON: That Lisa Bertram—she's no better than she should be. I never have liked you going round with her.

MR RICHARDSON: You heard what your mother said. Go upstairs and put on something presentable.

MRS RICHARDSON: That nice dress I bought you out of my catalogue. You've hardly worn it.

MANDY: But Mum, it's for a twelve-year-old. I'll be sixteen next birthday.

MR RICHARDSON: While you're living in this house, my girl, you'll do as you're told. Now go on, upstairs and change.

MANDY: O.K., thanks for ruining my evening.

MR RICHARDSON: One more thing. We'll have you back here by eleven o'clock as usual.

MANDY: Eleven o'clock! But the party will hardly have

warmed up by then. Warren never has to be home by eleven. He didn't come back till three o'clock this morning. He woke me up.

MRS RICHARDSON: He's older than you and he's a boy. You'll be back in this house by eleven o'clock or there'll be no more parties for you, my girl.

MANDY: Why can Warren do as he likes and not me? I have to dress like a twelve-year-old and you let Warren go out looking like something out of Oxfam. I'm not allowed make-up, or a decent hair-do and I have to be back home when everyone else is enjoying themselves. I might as well stay at home and listen to records.

MR RICHARDSON: And that's another thing. Your mother and I are sick and tired of hearing that din coming from your bedroom night after night.

MRS RICHARDSON: If you can't play your records more quietly, we'll have to take that music centre out of your bedroom.

MANDY: Warren plays his guitar much more loudly than I play my records.

MRS RICHARDSON: And if you are spending the evening in your room, you can tidy it up. That place is a disgrace.

MANDY: It's perfect compared to Warren's. Anyway, I think I will go to the party after all. Lisa's my best friend. I can't let her down after I've promised, even if I will look a freak!

MRS RICHARDSON: You'll look very nice after you've scraped off that make-up and put on a pretty dress.

(Mandy goes out)

MRS RICHARDSON: Stan, what have we done wrong? I just don't understand that girl. She's not a bit like Warren.

MR RICHARDSON: She certaintly doesn't appreciate all we've done for her. You work for years to give your kids a good home and this is all the thanks we get.

MRS RICHARDSON: I don't know what the world's coming to, if Mandy's typical of the younger generation.

MR RICHARDSON: No backbone, no guts, no respect for their elders. Thank goodness we've got Warren.

MRS RICHARDSON: He's a good lad, is our Warren.

MR RICHARDSON: Is there anything on the telly tonight?

MRS RICHARDSON: Not much. There's that detective thing you like at eight o'clock; then there's only the news and documentaries.

MR RICHARDSON: How about popping down to the pub later?

MRS RICHARDSON: That's all right by me, as long as we're back before eleven. I want to make sure that Mandy gets home on time.

Scene II

Lisa's house
Lisa, Clive, Mandy, Steve

MANDY: Hi, Lisa. Sorry I'm late—parent trouble.

LISA: So I see. Mum's choice of dress?

MANDY: Mum's choice of dress. Isn't it awful!

CLIVE: What the well-dressed teenybopper is wearing.

MANDY: Shut up, Clive. It's bad enough having to wear it, without having to put up with your comments as well.

LISA: Clive's brought a friend—Steve.

MANDY: Hi, Steve.

LISA: Steve's a roadie for a pop group!

MANDY: A roadie? That sounds exciting. What group?

STEVE: It isn't as exciting as everyone thinks. Sometimes it's just sheer hard work.

CLIVE: He's not with just one group. He works for a company that organises tours for groups.

STEVE: That means the groups we handle are usually the sort of up-and-coming ones, or the kind that make one record and vanish. Nobody famous.

LISA: What happened to your new hair-do?

MANDY: My Dad made me wash it all out.

STEVE: Mum's choice of dress, Dad's hair-do. You don't get much say in things at your house, do you?

LISA: It's a miracle she's here at all.

CLIVE: Warren doesn't seem to have the same problem.

MANDY: The sun rises and sets on our Warren. I don't seem to be able to do anything right.

STEVE: Perhaps it's just their way of showing that they care for you.

MANDY: I wish they'd find another way of showing it, then. I have to be home by eleven.

LISA: On my birthday.

CLIVE: That's a bit steep—especially when we haven't even got school tomorrow.

STEVE: School? Are you girls still at school?

LISA: In our last term. Why? Do you think you're cradle-snatching?

MANDY: One more term and we'll join the dole queue like Warren.

LISA: Don't be daft, Mandy. You'll pass your 'O' levels and get a job. She's got the highest shorthand speed in the class!

STEVE: Shorthand and typing, I suppose.

MANDY: You can't have one without the other.

STEVE: I might be able to find you something with our firm. Keep in touch.

CLIVE: Hey, you two, this is a party—not an employment agency. Come on, Lisa, let's dance.

STEVE: I'll sit this one out if Mandy will join me.

LISA: Don't let us get in your way.

(Clive and Lisa go out)

STEVE: Is it really as bad as you say it is at home?

MANDY: Every bit. But what can I do? I haven't got anywhere to go. I'll just have to put up with it.

STEVE: Once you get a job, though, you'll be able to leave home.

MANDY: IF I get a job.

STEVE: You'll get a job. But, tell me something about yourself.

MANDY: Nearly sixteen, still at school.

STEVE: No hobbies? No boyfriend?

MANDY: Plenty of hobbies—all sporty. But no boyfriend. Are you kidding, with my parents? They scare away every boy I meet.

STEVE: It takes a lot to scare me!

Scene III

Mandy's birthday party. Two months later.
Mandy, Mrs Richardson, Mr Richardson

MRS RICHARDSON: Now, I've got bridge rolls, sausages on sticks and those nice open sandwiches.

MANDY: Mum, nobody ever eats at parties.

MR RICHARDSON: Then they'll have some of this fruit cup. Taste it, Mandy.

MANDY: Couldn't we have just one bottle of cider in it, Dad?

MRS RICHARDSON: You know it's only your sixteenth birthday, Mandy. You're not allowed to drink until you're eighteen. We're not going to encourage young people to break the law.

MANDY: Just a little cider.

MR RICHARDSON: Once you start with things like that, you don't know where you'll end up!

MANDY: You're right, Dad. Look at Warren.

MRS RICHARDSON: What do you mean—look at Warren?

MANDY: Well I suppose he started with cider, but it was your whisky that he pinched out of the cupboard.

MR RICHARDSON: What is the girl talking about?

MRS RICHARDSON: Let me see. The whisky HAS gone. Mandy, what is going on?

MANDY: I told you. Warren nicked a bottle of whisky out of that cupboard last week. He'd spent all his dole money.

MR RICHARDSON: I don't believe you. You're making it up.

MRS RICHARDSON: Warren would never do a thing like that. I bet you took the whisky!

MR RICHARDSON: It's that boyfriend of yours. I always said he was a bad lot.

MANDY: He's got enough money to buy twenty bottles of whisky.

MRS RICHARDSON: He's got far too much money, if you ask me.

MANDY: Nobody's asking you. But why don't you go and ask Warren about that whisky, Dad?

MR RICHARDSON: I'll go this minute. We'll soon get to the bottom of this.

(Mr Richardson goes out)

MANDY: Mum, can I talk to you about Steve?

MRS RICHARDSON: . . . 18, 19, 20. Yes, dear.

MANDY: Were you ever in love at my age?

MRS RICHARDSON: In love? Of course not. You're far too young to bother yourself with such nonsense. Now where did I put those serviettes?

MANDY: Mum, Steve's asked me to . . .

MRS RICHARDSON: Go and fetch some glasses.

MANDY: Mum, can I talk to you?

MRS RICHARDSON: That's typical. Here I am working my fingers to the bone to give you a nice party and all you want to do is talk. There'll be plenty of time for talking tomorrow, especially if your friends don't behave themselves. Now, go and fetch me the other table-cloth, there's a good girl.

MANDY: Mum, Steve's got me a job in the office of the company he works for!

MRS RICHARDSON: Then you'll have to turn it down, won't

you? It's all arranged for you to go back to school in
September to do 'A' levels.

MANDY: I don't want to do 'A' levels. I've got the chance
of a good job and I want to take it.

MRS RICHARDSON: We'll have no more talk about jobs—
it's 'A' levels for you. If only Warren had your brains,
he wouldn't be on the dole now.

MANDY: Yes, Mum.

MRS RICHARDSON: And while we're on the subject, I think
you should start seeing a bit less of that Steve. He's
far too old for you. Stick to someone your own age.
Now, I think we're nearly ready. Doesn't it all look
nice? Dad and I will be next door if you want us.

MANDY: Yes, Mum.

Scene IV

The Richardsons' house. The morning after the party
Mr and Mrs Richardson

MRS RICHARDSON: Mandy! Mandy! Your breakfast's getting cold. Where is that girl?

MR RICHARDSON: The kids have done a good job of tidying
up. You'd hardly know there had been a party here
last night.

MRS RICHARDSON: I expect Warren did most of it. What's
this on the draining board?

MR RICHARDSON: It looks like a letter.

MRS RICHARDSON: It is a letter—from Mandy. 'Dear Mum
and Dad, I've gone off to live with Steve. I'm not

breaking the law and I promise I won't touch drink till I'm eighteen.'

MR RICHARDSON: The ungrateful girl. After all we've done for her!

The Play: Points to Discuss

1. Are Mandy's parents being over-critical about her appearance?
2. Should boys be allowed to have more freedom than girls? Why?
3. Is it reasonable for parents to fix a set time for their children to be home?
4. Are Mandy's parents justified in the way they interfere in her choice of friends?
5. Why are parents frequently blind to the faults of one child and over-critical of another?
6. Should drink be allowed at parties for the under-sixteens?
7. Should parents stay somewhere in or near the house during parties?
8. Is it unreasonable for Mandy to try to talk to her mother when she does?
9. Do you think that Mr and Mrs Richardson will ever be able to understand why Mandy left?
10. Do you think that leaving home was the right thing for Mandy to do under the circumstances?

Parents: General Points to Discuss

1. How much do you think parents are influenced by what they remember of themselves as teenagers?

2. Do you think that parents sometimes cannot keep up with the fact that their children are growing up? Do you think that some problems between parents and children arise from the fact that a mother may not want to accept the fact that her daughter is becoming a woman, or a father cannot see that his son is becoming a man?

3. How much do you think parents want their children to compensate for their own failures in life, e.g. making a child have piano lessons because they always wanted to learn to play the piano but never got the chance?

4. If you do not get on with your parents what should you do to improve matters? Where does the blame lie?

5. If your parents appear to be stricter than others, how can you overcome this problem?

6. How many parental rules arise from a parent's real concern over their child's safety, e.g. time to be home, hitching lifts, motor cycles?

7. If your parents' attitudes arise from the fact that their religious or ethnic background is different, can you compromise with them to help you lead a less restricted life?

8. What are the qualities needed to make good parents?

9. Good parents have good children. Do you agree?

SOCIAL PRESSURES

We Can Work it Out

Characters

CRAIG
PAUL
SHEILA
MARION
LIZ

We Can Work it Out

Scene I

The youth club. Early July
Craig, Sheila

CRAIG: You've been out with Adam again, haven't you?
SHEILA: What if I have? He only asked me to go for a ride
on his bike.
CRAIG: Your Mum would kill you if she knew you'd been
on the back of his bike. You know what she thinks
about motor bikes.
SHEILA: What she doesn't see isn't going to hurt her.
CRAIG: Well, I don't like you going out with Adam.
SHEILA: A little bike ride isn't going to do any harm.
CRAIG: You're supposed to be going out with me.
SHEILA: But you haven't got a bike.
CRAIG: Just because I haven't got a bike doesn't mean that
you can go charging off with anyone who has.
SHEILA: You're being small-minded and possessive.

(Paul and Liz come in)

LIZ: I've got those old copies of *Jackie* you wanted.
CRAIG: *Jackie*? What sort of rubbish is that?
PAUL: Let's have a look. 'How you can turn your shaggy
locks into a fab hairdo in five minutes.'

CRAIG: What a load of garbage. People don't actually read this sort of thing, do they?

SHEILA: Of course they do. There's a lot of good stuff in there.

PAUL: Take a look at that model. I bet she's good stuff too!

SHEILA: Trust you to look at it in the wrong way.

CRAIG: Take a look at those models, though—skinny, over-made-up, they're fantasy women.

SHEILA: I wish I had a figure like that.

LIZ: I wish I could afford the clothes they've got. It must be fantastic to have enough money to dress decently.

PAUL: You're all right as you are.

SHEILA: If I could afford it, I'd have wardrobes full of clothes.

CRAIG: If I could afford it, I'd have a motorbike. Then I could pull the birds the way Adam does.

LIZ: No it wouldn't. A girl is looking for more than material things when it comes to a proper relationship with a bloke. Adam's always asking me to go out on his bike—but I know what he's really after.

SHEILA: I've just been out on Adam's bike and he didn't try anything on.

PAUL: A motor bike helps. My Mum won't let me have one—says they're too dangerous.

SHEILA: That's parents all over. Parents never want you to have any fun.

CRAIG: I bet those model girls go for blokes with bikes.

PAUL: Cars—not bikes. Cars are what really attracts the girls.

LIZ: If we looked like that model we could have any bloke

we wanted—and we wouldn't have to come down to a grotty youth club to find them.

SHEILA: We'd be rung up by fantastic millionaires and whisked off in their sports cars to romantic candlelight dinners in exclusive restaurants.

PAUL: If you looked anything like those models you wouldn't be able to eat anything at your romantic candlelight dinner.

CRAIG: Those girls must starve themselves to stay that shape.

LIZ: Here's someone who doesn't starve herself—Marion. Good old Marion—fat and frumpy.

CRAIG: If Marion's coming over here, I'm off. I have no desire to talk to the most boring person in England.

PAUL: Nor me. Come on, the snooker table's empty.

(Craig and Paul go off. Marion comes in)

MARION: Where are the boys going?

LIZ: They'be been waiting for ages to have a game of snooker. The table's just emptied.

MARION: They always walk away when I come over.

SHEILA: Nonsense, Marion, you're just imagining it.

MARION: Maybe I am. Want a crisp?

LIZ: No thanks.

MARION: Bit of chocolate then?

SHEILA: No thanks, Marion, we're watching our figures.

MARION: I wish I could. I just seem to put weight on and on.

SHEILA: Perhaps that's because you eat and eat.

MARION: No I don't. I hardly eat a thing. I didn't have any breakfast, then I only had a plate of chips at dinner

time. My Mum says I don't eat enough for a growing
girl.

LIZ: But you've got crisps and chocolate now.

MARION: Crisps aren't fattening. Anyway, let me tell you
my big news. My auntie's dead.

SHEILA: That's awful, Marion. Did you know her well?

MARION: Never met her in my life. She lived in Florida.
But that's not my main news.

LIZ: Go on, we can't wait.

MARION: She's left my Mum some money. So we're going
to Florida for the whole of the school holidays.

SHEILA: You lucky devil. We can't even afford a holiday
this year.

MARION: It's great news, isn't it? I can't wait to go. Have
you any ideas about what I should wear?

SHEILA: Bermuda shorts?

MARION: It's Florida I'm going to—not Bermuda.

Scene II

The youth club. Early September
Paul, Craig, Sheila, Liz

PAUL: Have a good holiday, girls?

SHEILA: Just look at my pale white tan. I swear it's rained
every day.

LIZ: What did you do? Where did you go? I didn't see you
round here.

CRAIG: I went to my uncle's up North. It was even more
boring than here.

SHEILA: At least I had a job for a few weeks. Now I can afford some new clothes.

PAUL: Must be great being a girl—you can spend all your money on clothes. I'm saving up for a motorbike.

LIZ: I thought your mother said you couldn't have one.

PAUL: She's changed her mind since the next-door neighbour's kid got one. Everything next door gets—she has to have.

LIZ: That's stupid. What happens if next-door's kid dyes his hair purple?

PAUL: It's only things that my Mum copies from next door.

LIZ: I suppose my Mum is almost as daft with her ideas about school.

CRAIG: What sort of ideas has she got?

LIZ: She made me do school work in the holidays.

PAUL: What a right little swot we have here.

CRAIG: School work in the holidays? I don't do any in term time.

LIZ: She's got this stupid idea in her head that I should do 'O' levels. Would you believe she bought me books of past papers for me to work on?

SHEILA: Who marked them?

LIZ: That's the big laugh. She and Dad are still trying to work out the answers.

CRAIG: Hey, get a load of that bird who's just come in!

SHEILA: Who is she? I haven't seen her round here before.

LIZ: She looks kind of familiar.

PAUL: But what a figure! And that tan!

SHEILA: Those clothes!

LIZ: The make-up!

PAUL: Excuse me girls, I think it's time we went over and introduced ourselves.

(Craig and Paul go off)

SHEILA: You and half a dozen others! Isn't it disgusting the way that they're all swarming round that girl?

LIZ: Neglecting us into the bargain. What's she got that we haven't got?

SHEILA: I'll tell you: clothes, looks, a figure, a tan and from all that—money!

LIZ: Money. If we only had some money we'd have the boys swarming round us.

SHEILA: Who wants them anyway?

LIZ: I suppose if the lot here are all we can get, then we can't be very choosy.

SHEILA: You're right. But what is a girl like that doing in a dump like this?

LIZ: It beats me, but I still think there's something familiar about her.

SHEILA: I must say, even our honoured leader is being familiar with her. Look at the way he's leering at her.

LIZ: I can't bear to watch. It's too disgusting.

SHEILA: Let's turn our backs on the whole sordid scene.

LIZ: And to think that my Mum says that the only way to get on in life is to do well in exams.

SHEILA: Mine seems to think that life consists of doing your homework and coming home early.

LIZ: Parents don't have a clue about life, do they?

SHEILA: Just because they're past it they don't realise that we have our lives still to lead.

LIZ: We're not having much of a life, stuck here in this crummy hall while that glamourpuss hogs our blokes.

SHEILA: Something funny's going on over there.

LIZ: I'll say there is, and I've lost my sense of humour

where that dolly bird is concerned. I thought we weren't supposed to be looking.

SHEILA: I couldn't resist a peek. And look, all those blokes who were buzzing round her are all drifting away again. Paul's coming back here on his own.

(Paul comes in)

LIZ: Slumming, are you?

SHEILA: New girl given you the brush-off?

PAUL: Brush-off? Don't you recognize her? Put two stones back on, forget about the tan and the clothes and you have. . . .

LIZ: Marion! I told you she looked familiar.

PAUL: And she's got Craig well and truly hooked. The liar said that he'd fancied her for years. Look at them! Doesn't it make you sick?

SHEILA: Right, Craig. That's it, you've done it this time.

LIZ: Where are you going, Sheila?

SHEILA: I'm going off with Adam on his bike and I'm not coming back. At least he wants me for myself and not for my appearance.

The Play: Points to Discuss

1. Why do we value material possessions so much?

2. Sheila and Liz discuss what they would do if they had money. Can money buy happiness?

3. 'Parents don't have a clue about life.'
   'Parents never want you to have fun.'
   To what extent are these statements true?

4. What makes the Marions of this world so boring? Can they ever become interesting?

5. Is the change in Marion believable? Can people really change that much or do they revert to type?

Social Pressures: General Points to Discuss

1. 'Slim is beautiful.' How true do you think this is?
2. How important are clothes to you?
3. Do you think that magazines like *Jackie* have too much influence on teenagers?
4. The chances of being killed or injured on a motor cycle are one in seven. Why do you think motor cycles are so dangerous? Does owning a car or a motor cycle make a boy more attractive to a girl?
5. What constitutes a balanced diet? (Obviously not Marion's!)

6. Can you judge people by their educational qualifications?

7. Should you make fun of people who are keen and work hard at school?

8. What makes a person interesting and attractive?

9. How much do you feel pressured by the world you live in, e.g. television, your friends, parents, etc.?

10. What is the biggest social pressure upon you?

With a Little Help from my Friends

Characters

BARRY EDWARDS
CLIFF
DEBBIE
KAREN
MR BENNETT
MR EDWARDS
MATTHEW

With a Little Help from my Friends

Scene I

At school, break-time behind the bike sheds
Barry, Cliff, Debbie, Karen

CLIFF: Come on, Barry, give us a puff.
BARRY: Buy your own, mate.
CLIFF: You'll give me a fag, won't you Debbie?
DEBBIE: No way. You owe me six already.
CLIFF: Karen, you'll give me one, won't you? Go on, just one.
KAREN: O.K., just one. That makes five.
BARRY: Why don't you ever have any fags of your own, Cliff?
CLIFF: My Dad would kill me if he found me with them.
BARRY: You have to learn how to be clever—know where to hide them.
DEBBIE: Blazer pockets are just the right shape. My Mum never finds them on me.
KAREN: My Mum doesn't even bother to check. She says if I want to kill myself, it's my own funeral.

(Matthew comes in)

MATTHEW: look out, you lot, Bennett's on the prowl!
DEBBIE: He's been here already.

BARRY: We waited till he'd gone before we lit up.

KAREN: Bennett's so blind he couldn't see a double-decker bus if it was right in front of him.

CLIFF: His specs are made out of the bottoms of milk bottles.

BARRY: Come on, Matthew, have a drag.

MATTHEW: No thanks, I don't smoke.

CLIFF: Don't be such a drip, Matthew. Come on—live dangerously.

DEBBIE: What are you, Matthew—man or mouse?

MATTHEW: I don't want to smoke. You've all seen the films about what it does to your lungs. I don't know how you can be so stupid.

BARRY: That's just a lot of propaganda. My grandad smokes forty a day and he'll be eighty next month.

KAREN: It doesn't do me any harm. I've got the school record for the hundred metres.

CLIFF: One little puff won't do you any harm.

BARRY: Make you one of the boys, then, Matthew.

DEBBIE: Girls fancy boys who smoke—it's more manly.

KAREN: Come on, Matthew, you can have a puff of mine.

MATTHEW: All right then, just a puff. Are you sure we're safe from Bennett here?

BARRY: Safe as houses. Go on, quick, before you change your mind.

DEBBIE: The bell will go in a minute. Come on, Matthew, be a devil.

MATTHEW: Ugh! You do that for pleasure?

CLIFF: It's not the first puff that gets you. Go on, have another.

MATTHEW: I don't really think so, thanks all the same.

KAREN: One more little drag won't do you any harm.

MATTHEW: All right. There must be something in it. You lot spend enough money on cigarettes.

(Mr Bennett comes in)

MR BENNETT: Matthew, what on earth are you doing with that cigarette?
BARRY: Blimey! Bennett!
MR BENNETT: Mr Bennett to you, Edwards. And don't try to hide that cigarette. I can see it. Matthew, I expected a little better from you.
MATTHEW: Sorry, sir, I was only having a puff of Karen's.
MR BENNETT: So you two girls were smoking as well?
KAREN: Yes, Mr Bennett.

(To Matthew)
I'll get you for this later, you little rat!

MR BENNETT: Miss Williams will deal with you. Go back to your classes.

(Debbie and Karen go out)

Matthew, I will overlook this aberration. But you have been warned. I'll be keeping a very close eye on you in future.

(Matthew goes out)

MR BENNETT: Right. Who else was smoking?
BARRY: No-one sir. Just me.
MR BENNETT: You know the school rules. This is the third

time I've caught you smoking. It's off to the Head
with you.

BARRY: But sir. . . .

MR BENNETT: Yes, Edwards, have you something to say
for yourself?

BARRY: Yes sir, look at your fingers. You smoke. I've seen
you smoking in your car and in the staff room. Why
is it all right for you to smoke and not for me?

MR BENNETT: You're under age.

BARRY: No I'm not sir, I'm sixteen.

MR BENNETT: It's bad for your health.

BARRY: If it's bad for my health, why is it not bad for
yours?

MR BENNETT: It's against school rules and those rules are
there to protect you.

BARRY: It's a pity they don't apply to the teachers as well,
sir. Then they could protect your health as well.

MR BENNETT: Edwards, I'm going to take you personally
to the Head. Not only have you been caught smoking,
but you have compounded the crime by your insuffer-
able cheek.

Scene II

The Edwards' house
Barry, Mr Edwards

BARRY: Hello, Dad, had a good day at work?

MR EDWARDS: Where's your mother?

BARRY: Gone to see Mrs Fowler in hospital. She's left your tea.

MR EDWARDS: Put the kettle on, there's a good lad.

BARRY: Of course, Dad. Here are your slippers.

MR EDWARDS: Blast. I've left my fags in the car.

BARRY: I'll go, Dad, it won't take a minute.

(Barry goes out)

MR EDWARDS: What's up with that boy? He's never usually as helpful as this. He must be in some kind of trouble.

(Barry comes back)

BARRY: Told you it wouldn't take a minute.

MR EDWARDS: Right, lad, out with it. What have you been up to?

BARRY: Nothing, Dad. Honestly, I'm just trying to be helpful.

MR EDWARDS: You've never been helpful in your life. Now what have you been up to?

BARRY: Have a light, Dad.

MR EDWARDS: Stop beating about the bush.

BARRY: Kettle's boiling. I'll just make the tea.

MR EDWARDS: Are you going to tell me what the trouble is, or am I going to phone your Headmaster tomorrow?

BARRY: I wouldn't do that, Dad. You might not like what you hear. The Head's got it in for me.

MR EDWARDS: I don't doubt that he has. And if you don't tell me what you've been up to, I'll have it in for you as well, with this bread knife!

BARRY: O.K., Dad, no need to get violent. I've been suspended for the rest of the week.

MR EDWARDS: Suspended? What for?

BARRY: Cheeking Mr Bennett.

MR EDWARDS: Pull the other one, it's got bells on!

BARRY: Honest, Dad, I told you the Head had it in for me.

MR EDWARDS: You're not expecting me to believe that they suspended you for three days for cheek. If they suspended everyone at your school for giving cheek, they'd have nobody left. Now, are we going to get to the bottom of this or are we not?

BARRY: Well, there was another little matter.

MR EDWARDS: Now we're getting there.

BARRY: Mr Bennett caught me smoking.

MR EDWARDS: Smoking? How long have you been smoking?

BARRY: About a year.

MR EDWARDS: Where do you get the money from?

BARRY: My Saturday job.

MR EDWARDS: You mean to say you've been smoking for over a year and you haven't had the guts to tell me?

BARRY: Of course not. I didn't tell you because I thought you'd blow your top.

MR EDWARDS: I would have thought a son of mine would have more sense than to start smoking.

BARRY: But YOU smoke!

MR EDWARDS: That's got nothing to do with it.

BARRY: It's got everything to do with it. Why is it all right for you to smoke and not for me?

MR EDWARDS: You're under age.

BARRY: I was sixteen a fortnight ago.

MR EDWARDS: You were under age when you started.

BARRY: But I'm not under age now.

MR EDWARDS: It's bad for your health.

BARRY: If it's bad for my health, it must be bad for your health as well. Worse—you've been at it longer.

MR EDWARDS: That's not the point. I KNOW it's bad for my health—but I can't seem to give it up.

BARRY: I remember last time you tried, Mum went back to live with Grandma.

MR EDWARDS: I wish I'd never started. That's why I don't like you smoking.

BARRY: But I do smoke, and I enjoy smoking.

MR EDWARDS: What do you enjoy? Smoking—or the thrill of sneaking a quick puff in the toilets? Looking big in front of the girls? Wait a few years, it all becomes a drag—an expensive habit that you just can't kick.

BARRY: O.K., but let me choose. It's my life, isn't it?

MR EDWARDS: What do you think you're doing?

BARRY: Lighting a fag. It's one of mine—I haven't nicked any of yours.

MR EDWARDS: That's not the point. I'm not having you smoking in this house. You can smoke if you like— but not in front of me and not at school. Do you understand?

BARRY: Yes, Dad. I quite understand. I'm putting this cigarette out. I'm giving up smoking now this minute. Here, you can have the rest of the packet.

MR EDWARDS: That's great son. I'm glad I've made you see sense.

BARRY: You haven't made me see sense. But you've made me see that smoking has another health risk that they don't mention on the packets. You and Mr Bennett—

you've lost all reason. I'm giving up before I become
a blooming hypocrite as well!

The Play: Points to Discuss

1. Do many schoolchildren smoke?
2. Why do people smoke at school?
3. Do you think many people are pressured into smoking?
4. Should schools take a more tolerant attitude towards pupils smoking? For example, should they provide smoking rooms for the over-sixteens?
5. Should teachers and parents set a better example about smoking?

Smoking: General Points to Discuss

FACT: Of all the people in this room who now smoke, 25 per cent of them will be dead by the age of fifty, killed by a smoking-related disease.

1. Cigarette smoking is dangerous. But are the government being hypocritical in their attitude by not being stricter about the sale of cigarettes?
2. Do you think it is ridiculous that one can buy cigarettes at the age of sixteen but not legally buy alcohol until the age of eighteen?
3. Many of you have bought cigarettes before you were sixteen either for yourself or for your parents. Do you think this is right? Should the law be more strictly enforced?
4. What do you think about the recent spread of 'No Smoking' areas in public places?

DRINKING

I've had a Drink or Two and I Don't Care

Characters

MAX
DARREN
ROB
TIM
JOANNE
BRENDA
MR PARKER
POLICEMAN

I've had a Drink or Two and I Don't Care

Scene I

The dressing room after the match
Mr Parker, Darren, Tim, Rob, Max

MR PARKER: Well done, lads! You made it—unbeaten all season!

MAX: They nearly had us today, though, Mr Parker.

MR PARKER: Darren's goalkeeping did it. That last save— I've never seen anything like it.

DARREN: I surprised myself, Mr Parker. I didn't think I could hold on to it.

ROB: But you did, Darren, you did.

MR PARKER: Do you think you'll be able to keep it up next season, lads?

MAX: Sure thing, Mr Parker. We've got a winning team there.

TIM: None of us is leaving. But we have got exams.

MAX: We can win all our matches AND pass exams. Anyway, football's more important than exams isn't it, Mr Parker?

MR PARKER: I doubt that the Head would agree with you, Max. I wasn't going to tell you this, but one of United's scouts was watching the match today.

ROB: United!

MAX: Who was he interested in?

MR PARKER: He wouldn't tell me. Just said that he'd heard we had a winning team and wanted to have a look at you.

DARREN: United's goalie is rubbish. Might be a chance for me there.

MR PARKER: Maybe not United, Darren, but I've got it on very good authority that the lad who plays goalie for the county is being dropped and they're interested in replacing him with you.

DARREN: You're kidding, Mr Parker.

MR PARKER: I'm not. Max and Rob already play for the county—they'll back me up.

MAX: We've heard rumours, but we didn't want to say anything.

MR PARKER: Keep it under your hat. It all depends on how you play next season. Don't get too flabby in the summer.

TIM: We won't, Mr Parker. I'll be doing lots of swimming.

MAX: You can count on us all for the athletics team again.

MR PARKER: Glad to hear it. Now I must be off. I promised the wife I'd be back in time to take her shopping.

(Mr Parker goes out)

MAX: What about that, then—a United scout watching us!

DARREN: Goalie for the county!

ROB: An unbeaten season!

MAX: I don't know if you're all thinking what I'm thinking?

ROB: You bet we are! This calls for a celebration.

DARREN: 'Black Swan'—here we come!

TIM: But you're under age!

MAX: So what? Nobody bothers about that.

ROB: Are you coming, Tim, or not?

TIM: My father would kill me if he knew.

DARREN: Look, Tim, it's the celebration of a lifetime. You're not likely to play for a team again that keeps an unbeaten record all season.

TIM: O.K., I'll come but I'll stick to lemonade, if you don't mind.

MAX: Hear that, lads, he'll stick to lemonade!

Scene II

At the 'Black Swan'
Max, Darren, Rob, Tim, Joanne, Brenda

MAX: Come on, Tim, don't be such a wet. Have a beer.

JOANNE: It'll put hairs on your chest.

TIM: No thanks, I'll just stick to lemonade.

DARREN: That's right, Tim. Rob, get Tim another lemonade.

(Winks at Rob)

BRENDA: Are you lot staying here all night or are you coming up to the disco?

MAX: Look, love, we've had an unbeaten season, a United scout came to the match today AND Darren's probably going to be goalie for the county next season.

DARREN: We've got a lot of celebrating to do!

JOANNE: The netball team's unbeaten as well this season, but we don't go out and get smashed about it.

MAX: Girls are different.

BRENDA: I'll say we are—we've got a lot more sense.

ROB: Here you are, Tim, another lemonade.

TIM: Thanks, Rob. Do you know, I'm still thirsty after that game. Hey, this lemonade's got a funny taste!

ROB: They'd run out of the usual make. That's a different brand—that's all.

JOANNE: What are you up to?

ROB: I put a double vodka in Tim's lemonade. Now watch the fun!

BRENDA: You're just stupid you lot. So you're not coming to the disco, then?

MAX: Not till closing time. Then we won't be dancing— we'll be floating.

DARREN: Legless, we'll be!

ROB: Save a dance for me, Joanne.

JOANNE: They won't even let you in. Come on, Brenda, we know where we're not wanted.

BRENDA: We can't compete with a pint of beer. Let's go and find some blokes who'll appreciate us for ourselves.

(Brenda and Joanne go out)

MAX: Watch you don't trip over their white sticks!

DARREN: Thank goodness they've gone. Quite takes the pleasure out of drinking, doesn't it—having them looking down their noses all the time.

MAX: My round, I think. Another lemonade, Tim?

TIM: Yes please. Make sure it's the same make as the last one. I like the taste.

ROB: I'll bet you do.

TIM: It's so refreshing—so relaxing.

ROB: You sound like an ad on the telly.

TIM: That's an idea. Ladies and gentlemen—allow me to introduce you to the new lemonade. . .!

ROB: Shut up, Tim, everybody's looking at you!

DARREN: Come on, Tim, what's got into you? I thought you were the shy one.

TIM: Somehow I don't feel shy tonight. It must be the excitement of winning.

MAX: More likely the vodka. Come on, Tim, get that down you!

TIM: A toast. To the team. We are the champions!

DARREN: Go easy on that lemonade, Tim. You've downed that glass in a single gulp.

TIM: Single gulp. Superman Tim—able to down glasses in a single gulp.

ROB: Just drink that lemonade a bit slower.

TIM: Lemonade doesn't do you any harm. Who are you to tell me what to do? Just because you're the goalie, you're not perfect. Nobody bosses me around, see. I'll show you who's the boss around here. Stand up. Come on, stand up. I'll show you who's boss.

ROB: Come on, Tim, sit down.

TIM: Don't you tell me what to do either. Just because I haven't been picked to play for the county you all think you're better than me. I'll show you who's better.

DARREN: Be quiet, Tim, or you'll get us chucked out of here.

TIM: I don't care if we get out chucked. I'll tackle anyone who tries to chuck me out.

MAX: Come on, lads, let's get him out of here.

TIM: What are you doing? Why are you spinning the room around? Get your hands off me! Oh dear . . . I don't feel very well. I think I'm going to be. . . .

(Tims runs out)

DARREN: What a laugh! I bet that's put him off lemonade for a while.

ROB: Do you think he'll be all right?

MAX: Of course he will be. Come on, we're wasting valuable drinking time. Who's round is it?

Scene III

The pub car park. Closing time
Darren, Max, Rob

DARREN: We are the champions!

ROB: Hey, who's moving the car park? Tell the car park to stand still!

MAX: Must be an earthquake!

DARREN: Did you get those cans, Max?

MAX: Yes, here they are. 1, 2, 3, 5—something like that. Can't go thirsty at the disco.

ROB: Rotten disco. No beer. Only girls.

DARREN: Girls! Better than beer.

MAX: No closing time for girls!

ROB: Come on, let's see how many we can grab.

DARREN: I fancy that Brenda.

MAX: Hands off, she's mine.

DARREN: Joanne, then.

ROB: Keep off. I'm having her.

DARREN: Give us a can, then.

MAX: Here they are. Little beauties. One for you, one for you and one for me.

DARREN: Let's have another one!

MAX: Don't be greedy, they've got to last a long time.

DARREN: Go on, give us another one. Want to play the drums. Look.

ROB: Sounds better on metal. Let's try it out on a car.

MAX: We are the champions!

DARREN: Look—it's making dents in the car!

ROB: So they are. We are the champions!

MAX: Great sound. Got the beat. We are the champions!

ROB: Hey—put those headlights out, you're blinding me!

(Policeman comes in)

POLICEMAN: And what have we here? What are you lads up to?

MAX: Nothing, officer. Just having a bit of fun, that's all.

POLICEMAN: Bit of fun you call it. Vandalism I call it. Let's have a look at that car.

DARREN: It wasn't us officer, honest, it was like that when we came. I was just saying to my friend here, 'look at the dents in that car.'

POLICEMAN: Those dents just match those cans you're carrying. You can see that the paint matches—even in this light.

ROB: It wasn't us, officer. It was some big lads and they just ran away.

POLICEMAN: And look at those cans—all dented. Vandals, that's what you are!

MAX: Sorry, officer. It won't happen again.

POLICEMAN: I'll say it won't. Down to the nick with the lot of you. Into the car.

DARREN: Come on, mate, give us a chance. It was just a bit of fun.

POLICEMAN: Into the car—the three of you, now. We can discuss this bit of fun with your parents—if you have any parents.

ROB: Hey, who are you pushing around? Get your hands off me.

DARREN: I don't think I like that remark about our parents.

MAX: Shut up, the pair of you, and do as he says.

ROB: I'm not going to any police station. I'm off.

(Rob runs off)

POLICEMAN: Hey you, come back here! Get into that car, you two, if you know what's best for you. Your friend's in real trouble now.

DARREN: What's he done that we haven't?

POLICEMAN: Resisting arrest, assaulting a police officer—for a start.

MAX: But you weren't arresting us and he didn't touch you.

POLICEMAN: Don't you come it with me, sonny, or it'll be the worse for you.

DARREN: O.K., we know when we're beaten—even if it is for the first time this season.

The Play: Points to Discuss

1. Why do people use drinking as a way of celebrating?
2. Why should boys be more keen to drink and get drunk than girls?
3. Tim is portrayed as being rather weak because he does not drink. Do you think that is fair?
4. Why do we regard drunkenness as funny?
5. How do you view the role played by the police?
6. Do you think the policeman in the play was typical or not?
7. Do you regard the police as being for or against you?
8. What do you think of the present ways of treating young offenders?
9. How can the police play a greater part in the community?

Drinking: General Points to Discuss

1. The main cause of death in males aged between eighteen and twenty-five is drink-related driving accidents. Do you think enough is done to prevent drinking and driving?
2. Do you think the laws in this country relating to drinking ages are right? How should they be changed?
3. Is it possible to have a good time at a party without drinking?

4. Those people who do not drink at all, for religious, moral or health reasons, do you think they are missing something?

5. What do you know about alcoholism? What is the difference between getting drunk and being an alcoholic? Does one lead to the other?

6. Much violence in our society is directly linked to drinking, e.g. domestic violence, football hooliganism. Why do you think this is?

7. What do you think people should drink at parties: soft drinks, wine, beer, spirits?

8. What should you do if someone who has obviously had too much to drink offers you a lift home?

9. How much do you think that boredom and frustration is the cause of many young people drinking?

10. Do you think people would drink less or more if pubs stayed open all day?

Yes—We're Going to a Party

Characters

KATE
CLAIRE
LORRAINE
NICK
TONY

Yes—We're Going to a Party

Scene I

At the café
Kate, Lorraine, Nick, Tony

KATE: I can't stand that Claire. She doesn't half get on my nerves.

NICK: That's what I like about you, Kate. You're so kind, tolerant and understanding.

KATE: Don't you find her a pain?

TONY: A bit fat, dull maybe—but nothing to get myself worked up about.

KATE: She's always making up stories about these famous people she says she knows. I can't stand her.

LORRAINE: She's not as bad as all that, Kate. She means well.

KATE: You can say that again. She means to muscle in where she's not wanted. And she's always trying to buy our friendship Look at the presents she gave us all last Christmas.

NICK: I'm not complaining. If a bird wants to spend her money on me, I'm not going to stop her.

KATE: But you can't say that you really LIKE her.

NICK: I can't say I dislike her either.

TONY: Kate, don't you think you're going on a bit strong about Claire? You're being a right bitch about her.

LORRAINE: That's just Kate's charming way.

NICK: Why can't girls leave things alone? You don't find boys being bitchy, do you?

(Claire comes in)

CLAIRE: Who's being bitchy?

KATE: No-one. No-one at all. We were just having a discussion.

CLAIRE: What about? Can I join in?

NICK: Forget it, Claire.

CLAIRE: O.K. Anyway—have I got news for you lot!

KATE: Have you?

CLAIRE: My Mum's said I can have a disco—with a live band. My Dad says he'll pay for the hire of a hall.

TONY: That'll cost a packet.

CLAIRE: Money is no object, my Mum says. She says nothing's too much trouble for my friends. The group won't cost much. You see, my brother's got this friend. . . .

KATE: We know. The one who plays in the famous group.

CLAIRE: That's right. How did you know about him?

LORRAINE: You have mentioned these famous friends of your brother before, you know. There was also the disc jockey and the film star.

KATE: None of whom we have ever seen.

CLAIRE: All right. Laugh if you like. But if you come to my party—you'll see.

NICK: Don't worry, Claire. Just send us invites and we'll all be there like a shot.

CLAIRE: I'm writing them now. I've got so many to do— it's going to take me hours. I must be off. See you.

(Claire goes out)

TONY: What do you think about Claire now, Kate?

KATE: She's trying to buy our friendship again. Live group! Dead and alive group would be closer to it!

LORRAINE: Give her a chance. At least she's trying.

KATE: But the trouble is—she tries too hard.

Scene II

School. A few days later
Kate, Lorraine, Nick

KATE: Guess what I got in the post this morning?

LORRAINE: Don't tell us! An invite to Claire's party. I got one too.

NICK: So did I. But why did she have to post them when she sees us at school every day?

KATE: You know Claire. If there's a show-off way of doing something, she'll do it.

LORRAINE: Are you going?

KATE: Of course not. You know I can't stand the girl.

LORRAINE: But it's her birthday. You've got to go!

KATE: Who says I've got to do anything? And it isn't her birthday.

LORRAINE: How do you know?

KATE: When we were reading her horoscope the other day she said she was an Aquarius. This is September.

LORRAINE: I still think you should go. It might be quite a good party.

KATE: You can't be serious. Claire's party couldn't possibly be any good. She's no good at anything apart from pushing herself in where she isn't wanted. She's not one of our gang, no matter how hard she tries to get herself in. She hasn't even got a boyfriend.

LORRAINE: It doesn't mean there's something wrong with her if she hasn't got a boyfriend.

KATE: Then why doesn't she have one?

NICK: There was Mark.

KATE: He was a one-night stand. Look, I've had a brilliant idea—let's all boycott the party.

LORRAINE: We couldn't do that. Claire would be heart-broken if nobody came.

NICK: Don't be so soft, Lorraine. That's quite a good idea, Kate. It could be a bit of a laugh. How do we find out who else is coming?

KATE: We can guess. She'll have invited all of our class for a start. She said she had lots of invites to write, didn't she?

LORRAINE: I don't like it at all. If the whole lot of us say we're not coming, she'll just change the date.

KATE: That's the beauty of my idea. We all say we ARE coming, then we just don't turn up.

NICK: I think it's a great idea.

LORRAINE: I'm not sure about it at all.

KATE: Go on. She deserves it—trying to buy our friend-ship, always showing off, pushing in where she's not wanted.

LORRAINE: What if she phones up and asks where we are?

KATE: We'll all be out! Look, leave the organising to me. We'll have an alternative party—go skating or some-thing. Then, if anyone does phone, we'll not be home.

We can all say we made a mistake about the date.
Misread her writing or something.

NICK: You do have some great ideas, Kate.

LORRAINE: I still think it's a bit cruel.

KATE: Come on, Lorraine, make up your mind. If you
want to be her friend, be her friend, but don't expect
to be one of our gang any more.

LORRAINE: All right, I'll go along with it.

(Claire comes in)

KATE: Hello, Claire. How's things?

CLAIRE: Fine. Did you all get your invitations?

LORRAINE: Yes, thanks. You shouldn't have wasted money
buying stamps, though, you could have just given
them to us.

CLAIRE: I thought it was a nice touch. I didn't want to miss
anyone out.

KATE: Who else have you invited?

CLAIRE: Everyone. All of our class and some boys from
the fifth year: Alan and that lot. Are you coming?

KATE: Of course. Just try keeping me away.

NICK: I'm really looking forward to it.

KATE: Let's hope my Mum will cough up for a new dress
for the occasion.

CLAIRE: It should be a good party. The group's definitely
coming. They're quite well known. Oh, there's Mich-
elle. I must go and ask her if she's coming.

KATE: Don't rush off just yet, Claire. Can we give you a
hand, checking up on who's coming?

CLAIRE: Could you really do that? It would be a great help.

KATE: Of course. Nothing's too much trouble for my friend, Claire.

CLAIRE: That's really nice of you, Kate. I've got the list here. I'll make a copy for you during Assembly and we can get round as many as we can in Break.

KATE: There's the bell. See you at Break then.

Scene III

School. The Monday after Claire's party
Nick, Lorraine, Kate

LORRAINE: I don't know how we're going to face Claire this morning, Kate.

NICK: Saturday night was fun, but I feel a right heel now.

KATE: Leave it to me. I'll just say we all misread her writing and made a mistake about the date.

LORRAINE: Kate can talk herself out of anything.

NICK: I wish she had never talked me into this.

LORRAINE: Do you think Claire will ever talk to any of us again?

NICK: I doubt it. But isn't that what Kate wanted?

KATE: Stop being such a pair of miseryguts. Just leave it to me, will you?

(Tony comes in)

NICK: What happened to you on Saturday night, Tony? We missed you at the skating rink.

TONY: I didn't go skating. I went to Claire's party.

KATE: You went? What happened? Did anyone else turn up?

TONY: I went to the hall. It was a real rave-up. Dozens of people were there. I had a great time.

KATE: But I told you not to go. I told everyone not to go.

TONY: These weren't Claire's friends. They were all her brother's friends. The disc jockey and the film star were both there. And the group was 'The What'.

LORRAINE: They're in the charts!

TONY: It was a much older crowd. I talked to Claire and she said she was glad that none of you lot had turned up. It left the way clear for her to get off with the lead singer. And she did!

LORRAINE: Now who looks a fool, Kate?

The Play: Points to Discuss

1. Why do you think that girls are much more inclined to gang up on one another than boys?
2. What is the best action to take if you get picked on by someone?
3. Kate is a strong character. How are you influenced by people whose characters are stronger than your own?
4. What is the best thing to do when someone tries to impose themselves on you when they are not wanted?
5. How important is it to you to be 'one of the gang'?
6. Claire's stories were found to be true in the end. How dangerous is it to live in a fantasy world? Why do you think some people use this form of escapism?
7. If ganging up against someone causes real unhappiness, should parents and teachers intervene?

Friendships: General Points to Discuss

1. We all know people who are troublemakers. Do you think these people go on making trouble all their lives?
2. Examine your attitudes. How tolerant are you? Why do we tease those who are different, e.g. fat kids?
3. Why are we sometimes initially hostile to strangers?
4. Have any of you had an experience of not being accepted, or of taking a long time to settle into a new environment?

5. What are the qualities you look for in a friend?
6. Can you resist pressure from people who try to force you into doing things that you don't want to do?
7. How should you deal with people who call you names and spread rumours about you?

CRUSHES

I've Imagined I'm in Love

Characters

CHRIS
KEVIN
JACKIE
DIANE

I've Imagined I'm in Love

Scene I

Chris's house
Chris, Kevin

KEVIN: Come on, Chris, it won't kill you to have one evening out.

CHRIS: I'm not in the mood.

KEVIN: When are you ever in the mood? All you ever do is sit here moping, looking at Kate Bush posters, reading Kate Bush lyrics, listening to Kate Bush records. What kind of a life is that?

CHRIS: I like it; it suits me.

KEVIN: But it's not normal. You should be looking at real girls—not an unattainable pop star.

CHRIS: Just leave me alone, will you?

KEVIN: I've left you alone ever since you started this stupid craze. I've listened to those records with you, read those lyrics. Now I'm asking you to do something for me.

CHRIS: What's so important about the judo club anyway?

KEVIN: The judo club for me is what Kate Bush is for you. No, not really. I do go out with real girls once in a while. Anyway, I've told you this before, but you weren't listening. We have to raise money to help send the club on a trip to Germany.

CHRIS: Why Germany? Why can't you go and compete against English teams?

KEVIN: Because the German club came over here last year. They've invited us back there this year, but with half of us still at school and the other half on the dole, we need all the cash we can get.

CHRIS: How much do you hope to make with this disco tonight?

KEVIN: Not a lot—but every little helps.

CHRIS: So I've got to come along to your judo club and watch a bunch of dreary birds dancing, just so's you can go and booze it up in Germany.

KEVIN: You don't have to watch; you could always join in.

CHRIS: What's the point? All the girls we know are dull and boring.

KEVIN: Perhaps they are if you compare them to Kate Bush, but they are all we've got.

CHRIS: Count me out.

KEVIN: Oh Chris, I promised . . . I bet. . . .

CHRIS: You what?

KEVIN: I bet Steve Graham a fiver that I could get you to come.

CHRIS: You bet him a fiver? You mean you have to pay Steve Graham five quid if I don't pitch up tonight?

KEVIN: That's right. The club won't lose because whoever pays up puts the money into the fund for the trip.

CHRIS: All the same—a fiver! You must have been very sure you could talk me into it.

KEVIN: I wasn't sure. But it seems I was wrong. I thought you would have more sense.

CHRIS: What do you mean, more sense?

KEVIN: I thought you had more sense than to spend every

Saturday evening in here moping around about some pop star.

CHRIS: It's not that, it's just. . . .

KEVIN: You feel uneasy with real girls. You don't have to make any effort for a face on a poster. You don't have to talk to a voice on a record.

CHRIS: Of course it's not that, it's just. . . .

KEVIN: Prove it then. Come to the disco.

CHRIS: O.K., I'll come—but it's only to see the look on Steve Graham's face when he coughs up with that fiver.

Scene III

Diane's house. The same evening
Jackie, Diane

JACKIE: Honestly, Diane, I don't know what you see in him. He's at least nine years older than you and married with a kid. And what makes it worst of all—he's married to your sister.

DIANE: But he's not happy. He wishes he had met me first.

JACKIE: That's just what he tells you. You don't believe him, do you?

DIANE: He's not like that—honestly. If only you could meet him.

JACKIE: I don't think I'd like to. I'd give him a piece of my mind. I'd tell him straight what I think of him—making up to you behind his wife's back. He ought to be ashamed of himself.

DIANE: It's not like that, Jackie. He hasn't laid a finger on me. It's sort of spiritual, you know.

JACKIE: I don't know. There isn't a man born who isn't after all he can get.

DIANE: Garth's not like that.

JACKIE: Does Jenny know?

DIANE: Of course not. I'd rather die than tell her!

JACKIE: And I bet you haven't told your Mum.

DIANE: You know I don't get on with my Mum. I can't talk to her about anything. You're the only one that knows, and I wish I hadn't told you now. I wanted to share something pure and beautiful.

JACKIE: If you fancy your brother-in-law it's neither pure nor beautiful. The fact that he's nine years older than you makes it even worse!

DIANE: I thought you would understand.

JACKIE: All I understand is that you're making an absolute fool of yourself. Come out with me tonight. The judo club's having a disco to raise money. I promised Kevin I would go.

DIANE: Oh, you and that Kevin.

JACKIE: What's wrong with Kevin? At least he's single and my age.

DIANE: If you felt anything for Kevin you would understand how I feel about Garth.

JACKIE: I have to admit I'm not passionately in love with Kevin, but he's fun to be with and he doesn't try anything on.

DIANE: Nor does Garth. He puts me on a pedestal.

JACKIE: As long as he puts you somewhere he can't touch you, I suppose you're safe.

DIANE: But you don't approve, do you?

JACKIE: I don't approve of playing with fire, and that's what you're doing. Can you imagine what would happen if your sister ever did find out?

DIANE: But we're not doing anything wrong. He just talks to me in the car when he's driving me back from babysitting at their place.

JACKIE: He just talks.

DIANE: That's all he does. He tells me how marvellous he thinks I am and how he wishes that he'd married me instead of Jenny.

JACKIE: Doesn't he care for Jenny and the kid at all?

DIANE: He says that Jenny doesn't understand him the way I do.

JACKIE: Men have been telling other women their wives don't understand them since the days of Adam and Eve.

DIANE: But it's me that he wants. I've always admired him and now, he's the only one for me.

JACKIE: Don't be so daft. Come to the disco and meet someone your own age.

DIANE: You won't listen, will you?

JACKIE: I'm listening, but I don't like what I'm hearing. Now are you coming to this disco or not?

DIANE: Oh, all right. But it'll be an awful bore. All those stupid boys—but I suppose it's better than staying in watching the telly.

JACKIE: That's your Mum calling you, isn't it?

DIANE: What does she want?

(Goes to door and shouts)

Yes, Mum, I'm here. What? Jenny's on the phone?

Wants me to babysit tonight. Tell her yes, of course. I'll be right there.

(Comes back)

Sorry about the judo club disco, Jackie, but I've got something better to do.

Scene III

Same evening. After the disco. Street near the judo club Kevin, Jackie, Chris

KEVIN: So you didn't enjoy it at all?

CHRIS: I didn't expect to. Boring, not a single Kate Bush record all evening.

JACKIE: You and your Kate Bush. Can't you ever think about anything else?

KEVIN: He only came tonight because I bet Steve Graham a fiver that he would come.

JACKIE: Did he pay?

CHRIS: That was the only good thing about the whole evening: the look on his face as he gave you the money.

JACKIE: I might try bribing Diane. She's got a stupid crush on someone as well.

KEVIN: Chris hasn't got a crush—it's more of a fixation.

CHRIS: Talk of the devil—here comes Diane.

(Diane comes in)

JACKIE: What on earth's happened, Diane? Who's chasing you?

KEVIN: There's a right maniac in that car over there. Look how he's taken that corner. He must be drunk!

DIANE: He's not drunk. That's my brother-in-law. Oh Jackie, it was awful.

JACKIE: What happened?

DIANE: He was driving me home after babysitting as usual. Then he stopped the car—just over there. And then . . . oh it was awful.

KEVIN: What happened?

DIANE: He tried . . . you know. . . .

JACKIE: You mean the pure and spiritual went out of the window?

DIANE: That's right. He tried to kiss me. Well I didn't mind that, then he started, well. . . .

KEVIN: Spare us the details.

DIANE: I didn't know what to do. But then I saw you lot coming up the street, so I just jumped out.

JACKIE: And that's the end of a beautiful friendship.

DIANE: I'll never babysit again for them as long as I live. Do you know—he didn't even pay me?

CHRIS: That's funny, that's really funny!

DIANE: I'm glad something amuses you.

CHRIS: Your brother-in-law tries it on and all you can think of is money.

KEVIN: I suppose it is quite funny when you come to think of it.

JACKIE: Anyone fancy coming back to my place for a cup of coffee?

DIANE: I could do with something after all that.

CHRIS: I'll come if Jackie's coming.

KEVIN: Well, well, well, what have we here?

JACKIE: Come on Kevin, we'll go ahead and leave this pair to get better acquainted. See you back at my house.

CHRIS: What do you think of Kate Bush?

DIANE: I like her. I think she's great. I've got all her records.

KEVIN: This could be the start of a beautiful friendship.

The Play: Points to Discuss

1. Why do you think teenagers have crushes?
2. What is the point in having exchange visits with teams from other countries? Are they really worthwhile?
3. How would you go about persuading a reluctant friend to go with you to a party?
4. If you have to have a crush, which is healthier: a crush on the unattainable or a crush on someone you know?
5. What would you do if your wife/husband was having an affair with another man/woman? (I'd kill him! is not an answer.)

Crushes: General Points to Discuss

1. What do you think is the main reason some teenagers have crushes?
2. What is the best action to take if you get a crush on someone you know?
3. How can crushes influence someone's life in a harmful way?
4. What should you do if you are sexually approached by a relative or family friend?
5. Why should girls be more prone to crushes than boys?
6. What would you do if a younger kid got a crush on you?
7. Fan clubs are big business. To what extent are teenagers being manipulated by the media?

8. How far do you think the average audience reaction at a pop concert is the result of mass hysteria?

9. Does the fantasy image projected by a pop group make teenagers dissatisfied with their own life?

10. Why are parents so often unsympathetic about crushes?

SEX

Such an Easy Game to Play

Characters

TRACEY KING
MR AND MRS KING
DAVE, *Tracey's boyfriend*
SAMANTHA, *Tracey's friend*
GARRY, *Samantha's boyfriend*

Such an Easy Game to Play

Scene I

Tracey's house
Dave, Tracey, Garry, Samantha

TRACEY: Come on, Dave, surely you can think of more boys to invite. What about Alex?

SAMANTHA: Ugh! He's got spots and bad breath.

DAVE: He wouldn't come anyway. He says parties are boring manifestations of adolescent behaviour.

GARRY: You what?

SAMANTHA: Go back to sleep, Garry, unless you can think of some more boys.

GARRY: Why should we bother? After all, the fewer boys there are, the more girls there will be for me and Dave.

SAMANTHA: Garry Spencer, if you spend the evening chatting up birds again, I'll brain you!

GARRY: Is Linda coming?

TRACEY: No, she is not. Just because she's got big boobs you blokes seem to think she's irresistible.

DAVE: It's not just her shape, is it Garry? I've heard about her from Peter Mitchell. He says that she'll. . . .

TRACEY: Shut up about Linda. I'm not having a slut like that at my party. This is my birthday that we're planning and I'm not having it ruined by you two eyeing up every female there.

DAVE: Sorry, Tracey, we're only joking, honest.

SAMANTHA: What about that new girl, Sharon?

TRACEY: I thought we were trying to find more boys?

SAMANTHA: She might have a boyfriend.

TRACEY: If she has, she's been a pretty fast worker. She's only been at school a fortnight.

GARRY: Sharon? The one in 5A with the lovely eyes?

SAMANTHA: You haven't missed much, have you?

TRACEY: I suppose she has nice eyes, if you can see them behind all that make-up.

DAVE: Miaow! Who's being catty?

TRACEY: I'm not being catty. And just to show you how catty I'm not being, I'll invite her to my party. After all, it would be a nice gesture of friendship.

SAMANTHA: That's another girl on the list. How many have we got now?

TRACEY: 1, 2 . . . 7, 8. Twelve girls and eight boys.

DAVE: Great. Close the list. If you and me take three each, Garry, that'll even things out for the rest.

TRACEY: Very funny. Can't you think of any more boys we can ask?

GARRY: I don't really want to find any more.

DAVE: Forget about finding more boys. They'll turn up anyway. You can choose who you want from the gatecrashers.

TRACEY: My Dad'll kill me if we have any gatecrashers.

GARRY: You can't have a party without them. I always say it's a rotten party if you don't have to call the police at least once.

SAMANTHA: Stop joking, Garry. Nobody's going to crash
    Tracey's party. It's just going to be a quiet affair.
TRACEY: With the next-door neighbours, we've got, it has
    to be a quiet affair.
DAVE: Are your parents going out?
TRACEY: Of course they are. I wouldn't have a party if they
    were going to lurk in the kitchen all night. There's
    some sort of knees-up at Dad's club.
GARRY: What booze are we having?
TRACEY: Wine-cup. Dad's special recipe.
DAVE: What's that? One egg-cup of wine to a gallon of
    lemonade?
TRACEY: Just about. So you'll have to bring your own—but
    be discreet about it.
SAMANTHA: Now we've sorted out the booze, let's get on
    with writing these invitations or it'll be your sixtieth
    we'll be celebrating—not your sixteenth!

Scene II

At the party
Samantha, Tracey, Garry

SAMANTHA: Cheer up, Tracey. It is your birthday,
    remember?
TRACEY: Have you seen Dave?
SAMANTHA: I haven't seen him since you cleared up that
    broken glass.
TRACEY: Don't remind me: Alex Duncan, smashed out of

his brains on two glasses of my Dad's wine cup. Has
he gone home now?

GARRY: Last time I saw him he was being sick in the flower
bed. But I think he was on his way home.

TRACEY: I don't suppose you've seen Dave either, have
you, Garry?

GARRY: Not a sign. It's so dark in here I couldn't see my
own mother.

SAMANTHA: Come on then, what are we waiting for? Stop
nattering about your mother and let's take advantage
of the dark. Put on a nice smoochy record, Garry.

TRACEY: If you do see Dave, tell him I'm in the kitchen.

GARRY: Will do. Great party, Tracey.

TRACEY: Thanks. I'm glad someone's having fun.

(Mr and Mrs King come in)

TRACEY: Mum! Dad! What are you doing home so early?

MRS KING: Your Dad's not well. We went to have a dance
and he's put his back out.

MR KING: What the heck's going on here? Have all the
lights fused?

TRACEY: No, Dad, it's just setting the mood.

MRS KING: I don't think your Dad's in the mood for all
this necking that's going on. Come on, Eric, let's get
you to bed and leave the young people to enjoy
themselves.

MR KING: I'm not sure that we ought to allow them to stay
here on their own.

MRS KING: Don't be daft, Eric, there's nothing going on
here that you weren't doing yourself at the same age.

MR KING: I hope so, Vi, I hope so. I can't see so well in this light. I'll take your word for it.

MRS KING: Come on. Let's get you upstairs, then I'll come down and make you a nice hot water bottle for that back.

(Samantha and Garry come in)

SAMANTHA: Hello, Mr King. Hello, Mrs King. What are you doing back so early?

MRS KING: Eric put his back out while we were dancing.

MR KING: I should have known I was past it. My dancing days are over.

GARRY: Don't say that, Mr. King. I bet there's life in the old dog yet.

MR KING: Not the way I'm feeling.

SAMANTHA: Can we do anything to help, Mrs King?

MRS KING: It's all right, thank you dear. He just needs to lie down. We've got one of those special orthopaedic beds. This isn't the first time that Eric's back has gone.

MR KING: The way I'm feeling, it might be the last. I don't think that even that bed is going to do any good this time.

TRACEY: Do you want me to call the doctor, Dad?

MR KING: Undertaker might be quicker.

GARRY: At least he'll have some nice hard boards for you to lie on, Mr. King.

MRS KING: We'll see how you are in the morning, Eric. No point in calling the doctor out at this time of night. Now let's get you up to bed.

TRACEY: There's plenty of aspirin in the medicine cabinet— I got some in specially for tonight.

MRS KING: Come on, Eric, the longer you stand on it, the worse it'll get.

MR KING: You're right, Vi. Sorry to mess up your party, love.

TRACEY: Never mind. Let's hope you're better in the morning.

MRS KING: Where's that young man of yours? He could give me a hand getting your father upstairs.

TRACEY: No idea, Mum, I haven't seen him for the last half-hour.

GARRY: Don't worry, Mrs King. I'll give you a hand.

SAMANTHA: I'll come with you. Tracey, you'd better stay down here and keep an eye on things.

MRS KING: That's right—you enjoy yourself, dear. Find somebody else. After all, it is your birthday.

(Mr and Mrs King, Samantha and Garry go out)

TRACEY: So everyone keeps on saying. Ah well, I suppose I could make a start on the washing up. Great party this has been—everyone enjoying themselves except for me. I've had more fun at the dentist's!

(Dave comes in)

There you are! Where have you been?

DAVE: Sorry, Tracey. Just passing through. Have to go. Can't stop!

(Mr and Mrs King come in)

MRS KING: How dare you! And in our bed, too!

Mr King: Come here, lad. I'll give you a good hiding!

Tracey: What on earth's going on? What's happened?

Mr King: We've just found your young man in our bed.

Tracey: In your bed! Sleeping it off was he?

Mrs King: He was in our bed with a girl!

Mr King: We've left HER upstairs getting dressed.

Tracey: Who was she? Dave—who was she?

Dave: Sharon.

Tracey: The one with the nice eyes. That's what the attraction was. Get out of this house, Dave Humphries. I never want to see you again as long as I live.

(Dave goes out)

Mr King: If I hadn't done my back in, I would have given that young man a lesson he wouldn't forget in a hurry.

Tracey: Oh, Mum, what an awful thing to happen at my birthday party!

Mrs King: Never mind dear. It's not as bad as all that. At least it wasn't you that we found up there!

The Play: Points to Discuss

1. Should the parents be somewhere on the premises when you are having a party?

2. Do you find that girls are really jealous of other girls' success with boys? And are boys equally jealous of other boys who score with girls?

3. What should you do if you have a problem with gate-crashers at a party?

4. What do you think makes for a good party?

5. Was Tracey right in her attitude to Dave after he was found with Sharon? How much forgiving and forgetting should there be in a relationship?

Sex: General Points to Discuss

1. When is it right to have sex?

2. Why is it wrong to have sex under the age of sixteen?

3. Is the idea that 'the girl is the one that suffers' still true?

4. What is wrong with saying 'No' if you do not want to have sex?

5. If a boy drops a girl because she won't have sex with him, is she well rid of him?

6. Do you think people are forced into having sex because 'everyone else is doing it'?

7. Is there too much emphasis placed on sex today in films, television, plays, and pop songs?

8. Do you think that over-strict parents will make kids react by acting irresponsibly once they do get freedom?

9. Do you think abortion should be available on demand?

10. What do you know about the health aspects of promiscuity?

SEPARATION

All My Loving

Characters

NICKIE
CAROL
SHOP ASSISTANT
PHIL
GRAHAM

All My Loving

Scene I

In the boutique
Nickie, Carol, Shop assistant

NICKIE: What do you think, Carol? Is it me?

CAROL: I don't like the colour much.

NICKIE: Do you think Phil will like it?

CAROL: If he hasn't seen you for six months he won't really care what you're wearing.

NICKIE: But I want to look my best for him.

CAROL: Try something else. What about this blue one?

NICKIE: Phil doesn't like me in blue. I remember him saying once that blue wasn't my colour.

CAROL: It's amazing you remember anything about him after six months. I can't even remember what Ian said six days ago.

NICKIE: Some things you just don't forget. Fetch me the red one—the one with the frill.

CAROL: I don't think they've got it in your size.

ASSISTANT: Found anything you like yet?

NICKIE: I'm not sure about this one, and my friend's getting me another.

ASSISTANT: Special occasion is it?

NICKIE: I'm going to stay with my boyfriend. I haven't seen him since he moved North six months ago.

CAROL: Here it is, but I told you, it's not your size.

NICKIE: I might get into it. I haven't been eating since Phil left.

CAROL: You haven't been doing anything much since Phil left. You've been moping around like a dying duck in a thunderstorm.

ASSISTANT: Faithful type are you?

NICKIE: Of course. I haven't looked at another bloke since Phil left.

CAROL: Isn't it sickening? They write to each other every day.

ASSISTANT: What do you find to write about? That's too small—you'll burst the zip if you force it like that.

NICKIE: You're right, it is too small. There's always something to write about: what's happening at school . . . you know. Shall I take the first one I tried on?

CAROL: Why don't you have another look? There might be something you've missed.

ASSISTANT: Does it have to be a dress? Have you looked at the separates?

NICKIE: Phil prefers me in a dress. He says it's more feminine.

ASSISTANT: I've got a few more in the stockroom. They're waiting to have the prices tags put on them. You can have a look at them if you like.

NICKIE: It's very kind of you—going to all this trouble.

ASSISTANT: It's no trouble. I know what it's like. My boyfriend's in the Army and I like to wear something new when he comes home.

CAROL: I still think you're wasting your money. He won't remember what you used to wear. Men don't notice things like that. You could wear that dress you bought for the school dance. You haven't been out since.

NICKIE: I want something new. Just because you think I'm silly keeping myself for Phil all this time, it doesn't follow that I should go and meet him wearing some tatty old rubbish.

ASSISTANT: Here you are. I think they're all your size.

NICKIE: These are nice, aren't they, Carol?

CAROL: I suppose so, if you like that sort of thing.

NICKIE: Come on, Carol, don't be like that. Aren't you happy for me?

CAROL: Happy? You're charging off two hundred miles to spend a week with a bloke you haven't seen for six months and you want me to be happy!

NICKIE: What's wrong with what I'm doing?

CAROL: What happens if you can't stand each other? Writing letters is one thing; actually talking to one another is something different. People change, Nickie. How are you going to feel if you get there and you find you've wasted the last six months mooning around at home when you could have been out enjoying yourself?

NICKIE: It won't be like that. With Phil and me there's something special—something different. How about this dress? It's something special too, isn't it?

CAROL: You could say that. It most certainly is a bit unusual.

ASSISTANT: Slip it on. It's one of those dresses that looks like nothing on the hanger, but once you put it on— wait and see.

NICKIE: How does this fasten?

ASSISTANT: Like this. It's a feature of the dress.

CAROL: You can say that again. Rather a way-out feature
    at that.
NICKIE: What do you think?
ASSISTANT: Very nice. Very nice indeed. It really suits you.
CAROL: I have to agree. It looks really good on you. Phil
    will love it.

Scene II

The railway station in Phil's town
Phil, Graham

GRAHAM: I don't know how you get yourself into these
    messes, Phil, I really don't.
PHIL: It was all your fault. You talked me into going to
    that party.
GRAHAM: You'd been staying at home far too much. It's
    all very well having a girlfriend—but not if they live
    two hundred miles away.
PHIL: So now I've got two. Josie will kill me if she finds
    out about Nickie.
GRAHAM: You could pretend that Nickie's your cousin.
PHIL: Oh yes? Sorry, I can't come out tonight, Josie, but
    I have to go out with my cousin. She'd never believe
    me in a million years.
GRAHAM: We could make up a foursome.
PHIL: Get your hands off. Josie's mine. But I wish I'd met
    her after Nickie had been to stay.
GRAHAM: Why didn't you tell Nickie you had 'flu or some-
    thing and put her off that way?

PHIL: Her Mum used to be great friends with my Mum. If
  I told a lie like that the first that would happen would
  be her Mum phoning up to ask how I was.

GRAHAM: Her train's late.

PHIL: That puts off the moment of truth for another few
  minutes. What kind of a friend do you call yourself?
  Can't you come up with any bright ideas?

GRAHAM: Bright ideas? I'm full of bright ideas. Remember
  it was my bright idea that got you to that party.

PHIL: That's what I mean. You got me into this—now you
  get me out of it.

GRAHAM: You'll have to tell Josie.

PHIL: I don't want to tell Josie. She'll never speak to me
  again. Graham—you don't understand. Josie is here.
  Josie is now. Nickie's in the past tense.

GRAHAM: But she won't be once British Rail bring her to
  this station.

PHIL: After a week, she'll be going back home again and
  I'm never going to see her again.

GRAHAM: So it's all a matter of timing. If you wait till the
  end of the week to tell Nickie, you'll lose Josie.

PHIL: And if I tell Nickie about Josie as soon as she arrives,
  what am I going to do with her for the rest of the
  week? If only our Mums weren't such great friends.

GRAHAM: Would Nickie really go bananas if you told her
  about Josie today?

PHIL: She's written to me every day for the last six months.
  You don't really think she's going to get off that train
  and say 'Phil, dear, you've got a new girlfriend! How
  nice!'

GRAHAM: How does she usually react to things?

PHIL: She goes bananas! She's even been known to cry if I'm five minutes late for a date.

GRAHAM: So she would make a bit of a fuss if you gave her the push now.

PHIL: That is putting it mildly.

GRAHAM: Then there's only one thing for it. You'll have to tell all to Josie as soon as you can and hope she understands.

PHIL: Do you think she will? Is she an understanding sort of girl?

GRAHAM: From what I've heard, she's very understanding.

PHIL: Why didn't you tell me that sooner?

GRAHAM: She's very understanding if you're one minute late, but throws a fit if you're two minutes late.

PHIL: How did I get stuck with a friend like you?

GRAHAM: Make up your mind about what you're going to do. Here's the train.

PHIL: Goodbye, Josie. I'll have to take the coward's way out.

GRAHAM: Can you see Nickie?

PHIL: No, not yet. Too many people. Yes . . . there she is.

GRAHAM: The one in the yellow dress, with the green suitcase?

PHIL: That's the one.

GRAHAM: Why didn't you tell me she was a little raver? Phil, your worries are over. Leave everything to me.

Scene III

Nickie's house. Ten days later
Nickie, Carol

CAROL: Come on, then, tell us all about it. What happened? How was Phil?

NICKIE: Oh, I'm not going out with Phil any more.

CAROL: You're not? After staying at home every night for six months you're not going out with him! I told you, you were wasting your time. What happened up North?

NICKIE: I had a great time.

CAROL: But if you're not going out with Phil any more, how did you have a great time?

NICKIE: When I got to the station it was all right at first. It was marvellous to see Phil again. Then that evening, I found we had nothing to talk about. When he kissed me there was nothing there. It was like kissing your grandad.

CAROL: You went all that way to find out it was all over and you'd wasted six months of your life?

NICKIE: It wasn't like that at all.

CAROL: What happened then?

NICKIE: I met Graham, Phil's friend. He's the most fantastic person I've ever met. I'm going to stay with him for Christmas.

CAROL: But Christmas is months away!

NICKIE: I know. But we're going to write to each other every day!

The Play: Points to Discuss

1. Do you think Nickie is really in love—or is she in love with the idea of being in love?
2. What point is there in making a martyr of oneself for a boy or a girl?
3. Is Nickie right in letting her boyfriend influence her choice of clothes?
4. What problems do you think people have in adjusting their relationships when they are reunited after long absences?
5. Is Nickie a believable character? Do you know any Nickies?

Separation: General Points to Discuss

1. 'Out of sight, out of mind.'
   'Absence makes the heart grow fonder.'
   Which do you think is true?
2. If a girl is separated from her boyfriend should she go out with other boys? And if a boy is separated from his girlfriend, should the same rule apply?
3. Should holiday romances be taken seriously, or is it better to end them with the end of the holiday?
4. What are the problems arising from getting romantically involved with a foreign boy or girl on holiday?
5. Nickie in the play wrote to her boyfriend every day. Can a friendship be sustained without frequent contact like this?

Man Buys Ring—Woman Throws it Away

Characters

MR AND MRS CRAWFORD
MELANIE CRAWFORD
SIMON CRAWFORD
SEAN, *Melanie's boyfriend*
WENDY, *Melanie's friend*

Man Buys Ring—Woman Throws it Away

Scene I

The Crawfords' house
Melanie, Simon, Mrs Crawford

MRS CRAWFORD: Your father's late again.

SIMON: He must be working very hard. He's always late these days.

MELANIE: His tea's ruined, Mum. It's not worth keeping.

MRS CRAWFORD: Just give him a few more minutes.

SIMON: Here he is now.

(Mr Crawford comes in)

MR CRAWFORD: Sorry I'm late, dear. Something cropped up just as I was leaving the works.

MRS CRAWFORD: You might have telephoned.

MELANIE: It's funny, isn't it—the way something seems to crop up just as you are leaving the works.

MR CRAWFORD: And what do you mean by that, young lady?

MRS CRAWFORD: She's right, Steve, you have been late back an awful lot lately.

MR CRAWFORD: So what? It's none of her business, is it? Where's my tea?

MRS CRAWFORD: Here it is—for what it's worth. You're so late it's all dried up. I don't know why you can't phone and let me know when you're going to be late.

MR CRAWFORD: I can't eat this. Take it away and get me something else.

MRS CRAWFORD: If you had been here at the right time, it would have been perfectly all right to eat. Food can't keep forever, you know.

MR CRAWFORD: Take it away and make me something I can eat.

MRS CRAWFORD: If you want something else you can make it yourself. I've got more to do with my time than run after you.

SIMON: I'll fry you an egg, Dad.

MRS CRAWFORD: You'll do nothing of the sort. He can fry his own egg.

MR CRAWFORD: Forget it. I'll have bread and jam—again!

MELANIE: I'm off now, Mum. I'm meeting Sean at eight.

MR CRAWFORD: Where do you think you're going?

MELANIE: I said, I'm meeting Sean at eight.

MR CRAWFORD: Have you done your homework?

MELANIE: Of course I have—and I helped with the washing up.

MR CRAWFORD: What kind of shoes do you call those?

MRS CRAWFORD: Leave the girl alone, Steve. These are her new shoes. I said she could wear them.

MR CRAWFORD: Well I say she can't. No daughter of mine is going out of this house with things like that on her feet.

MELANIE: But I bought them with my own money.

MR CRAWFORD: I don't care if the Queen paid for them—you're not wearing them.

MRS CRAWFORD: Go on out, dear. Pay no attention to him.
MELANIE: O.K., Mum. See you.

(Melanie goes out)

MR CRAWFORD: How dare you contradict me in front of the children!
MRS CRAWFORD: They're her shoes. She can wear what she likes.

(Simon moves to go out)

MR CRAWFORD: And where do you think you're going?
SIMON: I'm off to my mate's.
MR CRAWFORD: What mate might that be?
SIMON: Roger Bell.
MR CRAWFORD: Then you're stopping here. I don't like those Bells—shifty lot. If you can't choose your mates better than that, you can stay at home.
SIMON: But Dad, he's got a new computer game.
MRS CRAWFORD: That's right, Steve, I said he could go.
MR CRAWFORD: I say he can't. He stays here. Why on earth can you never bake a decent cake any more? This shop stuff is awful.
MRS CRAWFORD: I can't work full time and give you home-made cakes.
MR CRAWFORD: Nobody asked you to work full time. You know what I think about you going out to work at all.
MRS CRAWFORD: I know what you think—I've heard it all a thousand times already. But what with Melanie and Simon out at school all day and you working late every night, there's not much to keep me at home is there?

SIMON: If I can't go out, can I put the telly on? It's *Top of the Pops* in a minute.

MR CRAWFORD: We're not watching that rubbish.

MRS CRAWFORD: For goodness sake, Steve, it's only music.

MR CRAWFORD: Music! Bunch of long-haired yobbos making terrible noises. We'll have it on the other channel, if you don't mind.

MRS CRAWFORD: I do mind very much. I like *Top of the Pops* and I want to watch it.

MR CRAWFORD: So it's 'I want' now, is it? Since you've been going out to work there's been no living with you, Iris. You seem to think you can do what you like. This is my house and what I say, goes.

MRS CRAWFORD: It's YOUR house is it? then you'd better start spending a bit more time in it. While you're about it, you might do a bit of work as well. The bedroom needs redecorating and the bathroom's a disgrace!

SIMON: The garden's a wilderness!

MR CRAWFORD: Shut up. Nobody asked for your opinion. Look woman, you've done nothing but nag, nag, nag since I came through that door this evening. I'm going out now. I'm going to a place where I'm appreciated AND I'm not coming back!

MRS CRAWFORD: Good riddance!

Scene II

School. A few weeks later
Melanie, Sean, Wendy

MELANIE: So my Dad's gone off with this woman!

WENDY: The one I saw him with?

MELANIE: I suppose so.

SEAN: This is terrible, Melanie. How's your mother taking it?

MELANIE: Quite well, considering. They'd been at each other's throats for months—so at least it's quieter now with Dad out of the house.

WENDY: Are they getting a divorce?

MELANIE: I think so. Mum's gone to see the lawyer today.

SEAN: What's going to happen to you and Simon?

MELANIE: Nothing much. I suppose we'll just go on living with Mum.

SEAN: You can go and live with your father if you want.

MELANIE: I don't want! I couldn't live in the same house as that woman. Imagine he was carrying on with her all the time behind Mum's back. Saying he was working late!

WENDY: I thought Simon might want to go and live with his Dad.

MELANIE: I doubt it. Even if he did, Mum wouldn't let him.

SEAN: What's your mother going to live on?

MELANIE: She works full time. Then Dad will have to pay maintenance.

(Simon comes in)

WENDY: Simon! What on earth have you been up to? Just look at his clothes!

SIMON: Hide me, Melanie. I've been in a fight.

MELANIE: In a fight? Who with?

SIMON: Roger Bell.

MELANIE: I thought he was your best friend.

SIMON: He was, until he said that Dad had gone off with another woman. I had to hit him.

WENDY: Doesn't he know then?

SEAN: Shut up, Wendy.

SIMON: Know what? Here, what's going on? Why are you looking at each other like that?

SEAN: It's nothing, Simon. It's just that . . . well, hasn't anyone told you where your father's gone?

SIMON: Mum says that he's gone to live on his own for a bit because they haven't been getting on too well.

SEAN: Shall I tell him?

MELANIE: No, Sean. It's not your job.

SIMON: What are you all looking so guilty for? You mean Roger Bell was right? I don't believe it! Not my Dad!

(Simon runs off)

MELANIE: Come back, Simon! Come back!

WENDY: Now you've done it, Sean!

Scene III

The Crawfords house. A few months later
Simon, Melanie, Mrs Crawford

MRS CRAWFORD: I just didn't know what to say when the Welfare man came.

MELANIE: What's Simon been up to?

MRS CRAWFORD: Playing truant, that's what. Hasn't been to school at all for the last two weeks. Well, what have you got to say for yourself?

SIMON: Nothing. Don't like school.

MRS CRAWFORD: But you've always liked school.

SIMON: Not since . . . you and Dad. . . .

MELANIE: Are the kids teasing you?

SIMON: It's Roger Bell. He's got a gang on to me.

MRS CRAWFORD: That's no excuse for not going to school.

SIMON: But they've said that they'll beat me up.

MRS CRAWFORD: You're going to school tomorrow if I have to drag you there by the hair of your head.

SIMON: You don't care, do you? My Dad would soon sort out Roger Bell.

MRS CRAWFORD: You leave your father out of this. And you, young lady, get your head out of those books and get the washing up done.

MELANIE: Mum, I've got 'O' levels in a fortnight. I've got to get this done. I'm miles behind as it is. You shouldn't have got me that job in the Easter holidays.

MRS CRAWFORD: We needed the money. Now that your father's gone. . . .

SIMON: You talk about him as if he was dead.

MRS CRAWFORD: I need all the help I can get from you two. Books aren't going to help you.

MELANIE: 'O' levels are. Now, Mum, will you leave me in peace and let me get on?

MRS CRAWFORD: You'll ruin your eyesight. Why aren't you going out with that Sean?

SIMON: They've split up!

MRS CRAWFORD: What do you want to go and do a thing like that for?

MELANIE: I would have thought that you would know the answer to that one.

MRS CRAWFORD: What are you talking about? I don't like your tone of voice.

SIMON: Here you go again—arguing. It's just like when Dad was here.

MRS CRAWFORD: Any more cheek from you and I won't let you go and see your father this weekend.

SIMON: You wouldn't dare. Just try and stop me. I'd rather stay with Dad than stay here. He always buys me things. You never buy me anything.

MRS CRAWFORD: That's because I haven't any money. I don't know where your father gets all his money from.

SIMON: Irene's nice, too: she's a better cook than you are.

MRS CRAWFORD: How dare you talk to me like that! Let me get my hands on you!

(Telephone rings)

MELANIE: Saved by the bell!

MRS CRAWFORD: I'll get it. Hello? Hello, Ivy. Yes, the divorce becomes absolute this week. The children? They've been marvellous. I don't know what I'd have done without them. They haven't been affected by it at all.

The Play: Points to Discuss

1. How did the Crawford family problems stem from the discord between husband and wife?
2. Do you think that Mr Crawford went off with another woman because he was miserable at home?
3. Which parent do you sympathise with and why?
4. Many parents do not tell their children about their marriage breakdown. Frequently they are kept in the dark about the existence of another man/woman. Why do you think parents do this?
5. Children frequently become the objects of 'tug of love' battles. What do you think are the reasons for this?
6. Melanie and Simon were affected by the divorce. Does divorce lead to teenagers having problems with their own relationships?
7. Why do you think one parent tries to 'buy' his/her children?
8. Why do you think that Mrs Crawford, like so many other parents, tries to pretend that the children have not been affected?
9. Should children be allowed to choose the parent they prefer to stay with?

Divorce: General to Discuss

At the present rate, one marriage in four ends in divorce.
1. Do you think that divorce has been made too easy?

2. Is it better to keep the marriage going 'for the sake of the children' or is divorce under certain circumstances a better answer?

3. Are the present financial aspects of divorce satisfactory?

4. Why do you think that the children of divorced parents are more likely to get divorced themselves?

5. Why do you think that marriages between young people under twenty-one are more likely to end in divorce?

6. How easy would it be for you to accept a step-mother/ father?

7. Is there anyone who is opposed to divorce on religious, ethnic or any other moral grounds? Why do you support those views?

8. Has the present trend towards easy divorce weakened the concept of marraige?

9. Does anyone gain from divorce—apart from the lawyers?

Two of Us

Characters

SIMON CRAWFORD
MR CRAWFORD
MRS CRAWFORD, *second wife*
ROGER EDWARDS, *her son*

Two of Us

The Crawford household
Simon, Mrs Crawford, Roger Edwards

MRS CRAWFORD: Will you get your head out of that book and go and wash the dinner dishes?

SIMON: Why is it always me that has to do the washing up? Why is it never Roger?

MRS CRAWFORD: Do as you're told. I didn't ask for you to come and live here.

SIMON: No, I was stupid enough to think that I'd be better off with my Dad.

MRS CRAWFORD: If you don't like it here you can go back to your mother. I'm not forcing you to stay.

SIMON: Who would do the washing up then? Precious Roger?

MRS CRAWFORD: You know that Roger's delicate. He's got asthma. How is your chest today, dear? Have you taken all your treatments?

ROGER: Yes, Mum, but they don't seem to be doing much good. I'd love to help with the washing up, but I know that if I get out of this chair, I'll have an attack.

MRS CRAWFORD: Don't you worry yourself about anything, dear, just rest there quietly. There's not much for you to watch on the telly this afternoon is there? Shall I pop down and see if I can hire another video for you?

ROGER: Don't put yourself to too much trouble on my account, Mum.

MRS CRAWFORD: Nothing's too much trouble for me where your wellbeing is concerned, dear. Simon, you get on with those dishes while I'm out.

ROGER: If you are going Mum, see if you can get *Alien Strikes Back*.

MRS CRAWFORD: The man did say it might be in today. Right, dear, I'll try.

(Mrs Crawford goes out)

ROGER: I'm not going to let you watch my video.

SIMON: So what? Your mother will find something for me to do as usual. Is she always like this? Is that why you have asthma?

ROGER: She always has nagged a bit, but I don't think my asthma's got anything to do with it. I didn't ask to get it—it just comes on.

SIMON: I've noticed that it comes on strongest when you're asked to do anything. It also seems particularly bad on Monday mornings.

ROGER: What are you getting at? That I'm skiving?

SIMON: I'm not getting at anything—just pointing out a few facts.

ROGER: My Dad used to say that I was a martyr to my asthma. He understood. I don't think your Dad understands me at all.

SIMON: He's not used to it, I suppose. What's he like, your Dad?

ROGER: Nicer than your Dad. I really look forward to the days I spend with him. If I had the strength I'd do what you did—run away.

SIMON: Run away? You must be mad. Your mother dotes

on you. Look at me—I ran away to here. Your mother
doesn't like me. My mother won't have me back at
any price. Take my advice, mate, stay where you are.

ROGER: I don't need your advice. If I wanted your advice
I'd ask for it, and I'm not asking for it.

SIMON: O.K., mate, keep your shirt on. Well, those dishes
won't wash themselves. I'd better get on with it.

ROGER: Get me a Coke first. I'd get it myself, but you
know. . . .

SIMON: Your asthma. I think I'll develop something handy
like galloping breakers.

ROGER: What's that?

SIMON: I don't know. I just made it up.

(Mrs Crawford comes back)

MRS CRAWFORD: They didn't have the one you wanted so
I got you *Creature from the Black Hole*. You haven't
seen that, have you?

SIMON: That's a good film, that is.

MRS CRAWFORD: Who asked you for your opinion? Are
those dishes washed yet?

SIMON: Just going, Irene, just going.

ROGER: Mum, Simon says that I'm faking my asthma. He
says it's all pretend.

MRS CRAWFORD: How dare you say something like that!
My Roger's a martyr to asthma, a martyr. How that
poor boy has suffered and you have the nerve to stand
there and even suggest that he could be pretending.
Get out of my sight before I do something I'll regret.

(Simon goes out)

ROGER: Do we have to have HIM living with us here, Mum?

MRS CRAWFORD: We'll just have to do our best to put up with it, dear. We don't have to like him.

ROGER: I can't stand him. He's got a funny look.

(Mr Crawford comes in)

MRS CRAWFORD: Hello dear, you're home early.

MR CRAWFORD: I had to see someone in the neighbourhood so I didn't go back to the office. Had a good day, dear?

MRS CRAWFORD: Not bad. I've just been to fetch a video for Roger.

MR CRAWFORD: How's the asthma?

ROGER: I'm all right, thanks.

MR CRAWFORD: Where's Simon?

MRS CRAWFORD: He's in the kitchen helping with the washing up. I was just saying to Roger, I don't know what we'd do without your Simon—such a good boy and so helpful about the house. Isn't he, dear?

ROGER: Yes, Mum.

MR CRAWFORD: I'm glad to hear it. I thought he was looking a bit down in the mouth lately, but he is a lad who keeps his feelings to himself.

(Simon comes back)

SIMON: Hello, Dad. I thought I heard voices. You're home early.

MR CRAWFORD: I had a call to make in the area. I thought I'd come home and see how you were all getting on.

Not much fun having school holidays in this weather, is it?

SIMON: Irene manages to keep me busy.

MRS CRAWFORD: I was just telling your father what a great help you were and such good company, isn't he Roger?

ROGER: Yes, Mum.

SIMON: I'm glad you're pleased with my little efforts, for I only came in to tell you that I'd broken a cup.

MRS CRAWFORD: Don't you bother about that cup, Simon. Why don't you watch the video with Roger? I'll go and finish off in the kitchen. Come and give me a hand, dear, there's something I want to talk to you about.

(Mr and Mrs Crawford go out)

SIMON: It's all right, they've gone. You don't have to be polite any more.

ROGER: If you are going to be here, you might as well make yourself useful. Put the video on.

SIMON: Nice to feel wanted. Here goes. Nothing's happening.

ROGER: You haven't switched the telly on, you idiot.

SIMON: Sorry. I'll try again. Still nothing.

ROGER: Have you got everything plugged in and switched on?

SIMON: Let's have a look. Telly plugged in, video on. Look the clock's working.

ROGER: Stop it and start it again.

SIMON: Right. Stop. Start. Nothing.

ROGER: I bet you're doing this deliberately. You want to

get your own back on me. You're just taking advantage of my illness.

SIMON: Don't be daft. There's something wrong somewhere. It's not my fault.

ROGER: Let me have a look. I'll eject the tape and start again.

SIMON: Suit yourself. But I bet you don't find anything wrong.

ROGER: Yes I can. You've put the tape in the wrong way round, you idiot. Look, the arrows point this way.

SIMON: So they do. I'm a right fool.

ROGER: You can say that again. You can't even put a tape into a video machine. You break cups when you do the washing up.

SIMON: But there's something I can do.

ROGER: What's that?

SIMON: Cure asthma. I thought you said you'd have an attack if you moved from your chair.

ROGER: You little rat! I'll get you for this!

SIMON: Hey, that's vicious. Right—you asked for it.

(Mr and Mrs Crawford come in)

MRS CRAWFORD: Simon—what are you doing to my Roger?

MR CRAWFORD: Just a friendly wrestle, isn't it, lads?

ROGER: He started it. He hit me first!

MRS CRAWFORD: How could you hit a boy suffering from asthma?

ROGER: I think I'm going to have an attack. I can't breathe!

MR CRAWFORD: Pity about that. We won't be able to do what we've planned for tonight if Roger has an attack.

ROGER: It's not that bad, Mr Crawford. It's only a mild
    attack.
MRS CRAWFORD: I told you, Roger's a real martyr to
    asthma. He won't let it stop him doing anything. He'll
    soldier on.
SIMON: What have you got planned for tonight, Dad?
MR CRAWFORD: I thought we'd all go down to the Steak
    House for a bit of a celebration.
ROGER: Celebration? What are we celebrating?
MR CRAWFORD: Irene's got a bit of news for you. She's
    going to have a baby!
SIMON: That's great news, Dad. I hope I can learn to
    change nappies a bit better than I wash dishes.
MRS CRAWFORD: What's the matter, Roger? Aren't you
    pleased?
ROGER: Yes, Mum, very pleased.
MRS CRAWFORD: I'll go and get changed. You two tidy
    yourselves up before we go out.

(Mrs Crawford goes out)

MR CRAWFORD: What's the matter, Roger? You don't look
    very pleased. Aren't you glad your Mum's having an-
    other baby?
ROGER: I'm glad in a way. But where's this baby going to
    fit in? You've got Simon, Mum's got me. What's going
    to happen to us when this baby arrives?

The Play: Points to Discuss

1. Roger suffers from asthma. How far do people let handicaps like this influence their lives?
2. Have you any personal experience of a parent favouring one member of the family more than another? What can be done about a situation like this?
3. Mrs Crawford is two-faced. How do you deal with adult hypocrisy?
4. Mrs Crawford goes to hire a video tape. Are the rules on hiring video tapes too lax? How many of you have been able to hire 'X' rated tapes (and worse) without any trouble?
5. Simon has trouble operating the video machine. Are some people naturally clumsy with mechanical things?

'Stepping': General Points to Discuss

1. How far do you think the 'wicked step-mother' image is true in real life?
2. Why do you think it can be difficult to adjust in living with step-brothers and step-sisters?
3. What could be done by step-parents to make life easier for their step-children?
4. What can step-children do to improve their relationships with their step-parents?
5. In most divorce cases the mother usually gets custody of the children. Do you think this right?
6. Divorce often creates more problems than it solves. Do you think this is true?

7. Do you think divorce brings more hardship and unhappiness to the children involved than to the parents?